McGRAW-HILL READING

JUST THE THING

Activity Workbook
Level G — First Reader

Authors

Elizabeth Sulzby
　The University of Michigan

James Hoffman
　University of Texas at Austin

Charles Mangrum II
　University of Miami,
　Coral Gables, Florida

Jerome Niles
　Virginia Polytechnic Institute

Timothy Shanahan
　University of Illinois at Chicago

William H. Teale
　University of Texas at San Antonio

Arnold Webb
　Research for Better Schools
　Philadelphia, Pennsylvania

Literature Consultant

Sylvia Peña
　University of Houston

Contributing Authors

Lillian K. Boyd
　Detroit Public Schools

Bernard P. Floriani
　Delaware State Supervisor for Reading

Kay M. Kincade
　University of Oklahoma,
　Norman, Oklahoma

Jacqueline Kiraithe de Córdova
　California State University at Fullerton

Leon Lessinger, CEO
　Health Champions, Inc.
　Beverly Hills, California

George Mason
　University of Georgia

Kathleen Naylor
　Educational Consultant
　Brea, California

Karen S. Urbschat
　Wayne County Intermediate
　School District, Michigan

Nancy G. Whisler
　Richmond Unified School District,
　Richmond, California

McGraw-Hill School Division

New York　Oklahoma City　St. Louis　San Francisco　Dallas　Atlanta

ISBN 0-07-042077-7 FR

Copyright © 1989 by McGraw-Hill, Inc. All rights reserved. Printed in
the United States of America. Except as permitted under the United
States Copyright Act of 1976, no part of this publication may be
reproduced or distributed in any form or by any means, or stored in a
data base or retrieval system, without the prior written permission of
the publisher.

McGraw-Hill School Division
1200 Northwest 63rd Street
Oklahoma City, Oklahoma 73116-5712

4567890−8976543210

Reviewers

Marjorie F. Becking, Reading/Language Arts Specialist
  Orchard Park Central Schools, Orchard Park, New York
Jean Cleary, Reading Specialist
  Woodside School, River Vale, New Jersey
Lisa Sperling Fleisher, Director Graduate Program Learning Disabilities
  New York University
Margaret Haas, BVM, Curriculum Consultant
  Office of Catholic Education, Chicago, Illinois
Sarah Horn, Director of Instruction
  Bessemer City Schools, Bessemer, Alabama
Ruth F. Litchfield, Consultant
  Lexington, Massachusetts
John W. Logan, Reading/Language Arts Coordinator
  Community Consolidated School District 21, Wheeling, Illinois
Sandy McGilchrist, Reading Coordinator
  Federal Way School District, Federal Way, Washington
Linda G. Sherman, Comprehensive Reading Teacher
  Midland Public Schools, Midland, Texas
Helen Thomas, Director of Curriculum
  Elk City Public Schools, Elk City, Oklahoma
Lynn A. Torra, Reading Specialist
  Woodbridge Township School District, Colonia, New Jersey

Name _____

"Strange Bumps," pages 16–23

Endings

The letters **ld**, **mp**, **lp** make the ending sounds you hear in the words *old*, *bump*, and *help*.

Find the best word to finish each sentence. Write **ld**, **lp**, or **mp** to end the word.

1. Tim wants to be warm. _____

   But it is so co _____ out today.

2. Tim finds a rope. _____

   Can the rope he _____ Tim get warm?

   _____

3. Yes, Tim can ju _____ rope.

   That will make Tim warm!

To Do At Home Think of words that end with **ld**, **mp**, or **lp**. Write your words and show them to someone at home.

Decoding Skills: Endings *ld, mp, lp*

Name

"Strange Bumps," pages 16–23

Vowel Sounds

The letters igh can make the long i sound, as in *might*.

Write the word that has the long i sound to finish each sentence.

1. A sound in the _____ scares Meg.

    house   night

2. What _____ it be?

    might   could

3. In the _____ she can see it is just the cat!

    light   sun

To Do At Home Draw a picture that shows something that might scare you at night. Show your picture to someone at home.

Decoding Skills: Vowel Sounds /i/igh

Name

"Strange Bumps," pages 16–23

Contractions

In a **contraction**, two words are put together, but a letter is left out. An apostrophe (') takes the place of the missing letter.

Read the words in the box.

he is	he's	has not	hasn't
she is	she's	have not	haven't
it is	it's	had not	hadn't

Put a line under the contraction for the words in dark print.

1. **it is**
   a. its
   b. it's

2. **have not**
   a. haven't
   b. havent

3. **he is**
   a. he's
   b. hes

4. **has not**
   a. hasnt
   b. hasn't

To Do At Home Write a sentence for the contractions: *she's* and *hadn't*. Show your sentences to someone at home.

Study Skill: Contractions *is, not*

Name

"Strange Bumps," pages 16–23

Parts of a Book

Most books start with pages like these.

Title Page

The Owl's
Good Food Book

by
Otto Owl

Table of Contents

	Page
Time To Eat.	4
Night Food	6
Berry Dish.	12
Nice Mouse.	14

The **title page** tells the name of the book and who wrote the book. The **table of contents** tells what is in the book. It tells the page where each part starts.

Put a line under the right answer.

1. The name of the book is
   a. Otto Owl.
   b. The Owl's Good Food Book.

2. The book is by
   a. Nice Mouse.
   b. Otto Owl.

3. "Berry Dish" starts on page
   a. 12.
   b. 14.

4. The story on page 6 is
   a. "Night Food."
   b. "Time To Eat."

To Do At Home Think of a book you could make.
Write a table of contents for your book. Show
your table of contents to someone at home.

Copyright © by McGraw-Hill, Inc.

Study Skills: Parts of a Book

Name

"Strange Bumps," pages 16–23

Words from the Story

Read the words in the box. Then write the word that goes with each picture.

| bumps | bang | same | sat | rest |
| blanket | those | strange | cried | chair |

1. _____

3. _____

2. _____

4. _____

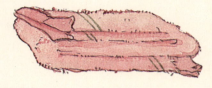

5. _____

To Do At Home Draw a picture that shows something strange. Share your picture with someone at home.

Words from the Story

Copyright © by McGraw-Hill, Inc. 5

Name

"Strange Bumps," pages 16–23

Understanding the Story

Read each question about "Strange Bumps."
Then write the answer on the lines.

1. What did Owl see under the blanket?

2. What did Owl pull from his bed?

3. What fell down when Owl jumped on it?

4. What are the things Owl is afraid of?

To Do At Home Write a note to Owl. Tell him
what to do if he is afraid in the dark again. Share
your note with someone at home.

6 Copyright © by McGraw-Hill, Inc.

Understanding the Story

Name

"Strange Bumps," pages 16–23

Endings

The letters **ld**, **mp**, and **lp** make the ending sounds you hear in the words *old*, *bump*, and *help*.

Write **ld**, **lp**, or **mp** to end the word that names each picture.

1. ju _____

2. la _____

3. go _____

To Do At Home Think of a word that ends with **ld**, **lp**, or **mp**. Draw a picture that shows this word. Show your picture to someone at home.

Decoding Skills: Endings *ld*, *mp*, *lp*

Name

"Strange Bumps," pages 16–23

Parts of a Book

A title page tells the name of the book and who it is by. The table of contents tells what is in the book. It tells the page where each part starts. Read the two pages. Then answer the questions.

Title Page

Animal Tails

by
Fred Frog

Table of Contents

	Page
Bears	3
Birds	7
Cats	13
Elephants	19

1. What is the name of the book?

_____

_____

2. Who wrote the book?

_____

_____

3. What is the first page of "Cats"? _____

To Do At Home Get a book. Find the title page and the table of contents. Show the pages to someone at home. Tell what each page shows you.

8 Copyright © by McGraw-Hill, Inc.

Study Skills: Parts of a Book

Name

"First Pink Light," pages 24–35

Words from the Story

Write the word from the box that is most like the words on the left.

| pink | light | hid | hide | late | leave |
| here | carry | studying | | surprise | |

1. not on time _____

2. go away _____

3. to hold _____

4. comes from the sun _____

To Do At Home Write about something that would make a good surprise. Show it to someone at home.

Words from the Story

Name

"First Pink Light," pages 24–35

Understanding the Story

Put **1** by what happened first in "First Pink Light." Put **2** by what happened next. Put **3** by what happened after that. Put **4** by what happened last.

_____ Tyree sits in the big chair.

_____ Tyree sleeps in the chair.

_____ Tyree's daddy is carrying him to bed.

_____ Tyree hides under the big box.

To Do At Home Draw a picture of a place where you like to hide. Show your picture to someone at home.

Name

"First Pink Light," pages 24–35

Vowel Sounds

The letters igh can make the long **i** sound, as in *might*.

Write the word that has the long i sound to complete each sentence.

1. The birds sleep the _____ away in the trees.

   night   winter

2. Each tree _____ have many birds in it.

   will   might

3. At the first _____, they all fly off.

   hill   light

To Do At Home Draw a picture to show some birds. Show your picture to someone at home.

Decoding Skills: Vowel Sounds /i/igh

Copyright © by McGraw-Hill, Inc.   **11**

Name

"First Pink Light," pages 24–35

Contractions

In a **contraction**, two words are put together, but one letter is left out. An **apostrophe (')** takes the place of the missing letter. Read the words in the box.

	Contraction
he is	he's
it is	it's
has not	hasn't
she is	she's
could not	couldn't

Write the contraction for the underlined words.

1. He is here. _____

2. They could not come. _____

3. It is cold. _____

To Do At Home Write the contractions for the words: *had not*; *have not*. Show the contractions to someone at home. Tell what two words each contraction stands for.

12 Copyright © by McGraw-Hill, Inc.

Study Skills: Contractions

Name

"Too Many Books," pages 38–45

Vowel Sounds

Long o can have the sound of **ow** in *throw*.

Write the word that has the **long o** sound to complete each sentence.

1. My friend will never _____ .

   look   grow

2. Do you _____ who he is?

   know   forget

3. If you like, I will _____

   _____ him to you.

   move   show

4. My friend is made of _____

   _____ !

   snow   wood

To Do At Home Draw a picture of something that you would like to show. Show your picture to someone at home.

Decoding Skills: Vowel Sounds /ō/ow

Name

"Too Many Books," pages 38–45

Compound Words

A *compound word* is one word made up of two words.

birdhouse **wild**cat **house**boat

Put a line under the compound word in each sentence.

1. We like this treehouse.

2. Everyone is in it.

3. It is on a hilltop.

4. A blackbird sings.

5. It is nighttime.

To Do At Home Write a sentence for each of the compound words: *grandpa*, *homework*, *daytime*. Show your sentences to someone at home.

Decoding Skills: Compound Words

Name

"Too Many Books," pages 38–45

Classifying

To *classify* is to put things together that are like each other. These things are like each other because they are all animals.

duck   horse   giraffe   kitten

1. Put a line under the words that name *a part of you*.

feet   drum   hand   eye

2. Put a line under the words that name *people*.

house   mother   baby   boy

3. Put a line under the words that name *food*.

egg   cake   berries   rocks

To Do At Home Write *Plants* on your paper. Draw pictures of three different plants. Show your pictures to someone at home. Tell why the pictures belong together.

Vocabulary Skills: Classifying

Name

"Too Many Books," pages 38–45

Comprehension Builder: Sequence

Read the story below. Use the notes in blue to help you think about when each thing takes place. Then answer the questions.

Watch what happens first in the story.

Jill found the book in an old book shop. It was a big, old book. There were many stories in it. Jill just had to get it.

At home, Jill started to read one of the stories. The first one was about a lion. As Jill read, she saw something jump onto her bed. Jill looked up. There was a lion in her room!

Jill got up in surprise. As she did, she closed the book. That made the lion go away. "How strange!" said Jill.

Look for clue words that show the order in which things take place.

Next, Jill started to read about a giant. As soon as she did, she could hear "BUMP! BUMP! BUMP!" coming from in front of the house. Jill looked out. The giant was too big to get in. But Jill was still scared. She closed the book, and the giant went away.

The ending tells what happens last.

At last, Jill looked in the book one more time. One of the stories was about an eagle. It gave people rides in the air. "This sounds better," said Jill.

(Continued)

16 Copyright © by McGraw-Hill, Inc.

Comprehension Builder: Sequence

Name

"Too Many Books," pages 38–45

Comprehension Builder: Sequence *(Continued)*

1. Which story does Jill start to read first?

_____

_____

_____

_____

2. Which of the stories does she begin to read next?

_____

_____

_____

_____

To Do At Home Imagine you are reading Jill's book. Tell about something that might happen to you.

Copyright © by McGraw-Hill, Inc.   **17**

Name

"Too Many Books," pages 38–45

Words from the Story

Write the word from the box that best completes each sentence.

| owned | room | small | called | fit |
| loved | library | give | aunt | learned |

1. You will find many books in the city _____ .

2. Many people have _____ _____ from books.

3. A _____ book may have big ideas.

4. A good book will _____ you lots to think about.

To Do At Home Think of a book that you would like to get from the library. Ask someone at home to help you.

Name

"Too Many Books," pages 38–45

Understanding the Story

Write the word that best completes each sentence about "Too Many Books." Then answer the question.

_ _ _ _ _ _ _ _ _ _ _ _

1. The books cannot _____ in the house.

    hit   fit

2. Maralou starts to give away some

_ _ _ _ _ _ _ _ _ _ _ _ _ _ _ _ .

    books   towns

◆ **COMPREHENSION BUILDER**

What words tell you the order in which things happen in the story?

_ _

_ _

To Do At Home Choose a book that you like very much. Show it to someone at home and tell why you like it.

Understanding the Story

Name

"Too Many Books," pages 38–45

Vowel Sounds

Long o can have the sound of **ow** in *throw*.

Write the word that has the **long o** sound to complete each sentence.

1. Jan and Dan _____ too many books.
   found   own

2. They would never _____ books away.
   throw   move

3. Their books seem to _____ all the time.
   shop   grow

4. Jan and Dan do not _____ what to do.
   forget   know

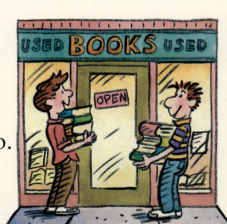

To Do At Home Write five sentences about your favorite book. Show the sentences to someone at home.

20 Copyright © by McGraw-Hill, Inc.   **Decoding Skills: Vowel sounds:** *long o*

Name

"Lizzie and Harold," pages 46–57

Words from the Story

Write the word from the box that is the most like the words on the list.

right	much	quick	told
stood	bell	her	thought

1. something that rings

2. fast

3. said to

4. rested on feet

5. a lot

To Do At Home Pick two words you learned in this story. Write a sentence using each word. Show your sentences to someone at home.

Words from the Story

Copyright © by McGraw-Hill, Inc. 21

Name

"Lizzie and Harold," pages 46–57

Understanding the Story

Read each sentence about "Lizzie and Harold." Decide if Lizzie said it or Harold said it. Write the name on the line. Then answer the question.

1. Today I am going to find my best friend.

2. Why do you want a best friend?

COMPREHENSION BUILDER

What happens after Harold says he likes Lizzie better than Douglas?

To Do At Home What do you think makes a good friend? Make a list. Show it to someone at home.

22 Copyright © by McGraw-Hill, Inc.

Understanding the Story

Name

"Lizzie and Harold," pages 46–57

Compound Words

A *compound word* is one word made up of two words.

Mail is a word.   Box is a word.

You can put *mail* and *box* together to make another word: **mailbox**.

Put the two words together to make a compound word.

1. kick   ball   _____

2. bed   time   _____

3. drive   way   _____

4. bus   stop   _____

To Do At Home Choose two of the compound words from the list you just made. Use each one in a sentence. Show your sentences to someone at home. Tell what the compound words are.

Decoding Skills: Compound Words

Name

"Lizzie and Harold" pages 46–57

Classifying

To *classify* is to put things together that are like each other. The words below name *places*. That is how they are like each other.

house   **store**   **school**

Read the words in the box. Then write the words in the group where they belong.

blue	sing	green	jump	red	swim

1. Colors to See

_____

_____

_____

2. Things to Do

_____

_____

_____

To Do At Home Draw pictures of five things that go together. Show them to someone at home.

24   Copyright © by McGraw-Hill, Inc.

Vocabulary Skills: Classifying

Name

Part One: Close to Home

Think about the stories you read. Use what you know about the stories to write sentences about the ideas on this page.

1. If I have to stay at home all day, I can think of a lot of fun things to do. The first thing I would do

2. I am happy with my best friend because

To Do At Home Think of a title for each story.
Read your title and story to someone at home.

Creative Writing

Copyright © by McGraw-Hill, Inc.   **25**

Name

"The Birds Take a Fall Trip," pages 66–73

Making Comparisons

To *compare* means to tell how things are different. To compare two things, add **-er**. To compare more than two things, add **-est**. Read the examples.

This is *warm*.   This is *warmer*.   This is *warmest* of all.

Put a line under the word that is right for the sentence.

1. She is ___ than I am.
   a. strongest   b. stronger

2. Tom is the ___ of all.
   a. faster   b. fastest

3. My book is ___ than yours.
   a. long   b. longer

To Do At Home Write a sentence using each word: **hard, harder, hardest**. Show your sentences to someone at home.

26 Copyright © by McGraw-Hill, Inc. **Comprehension Skills: Making Comparisons**

Name

"The Birds Take a Fall Trip," pages 66–73

Vowel Sounds

The letters **oi** or **oy** can stand for the **oi** sound in *soil* and *joy*.

Write **b**, **c**, **f**, **p**, **s**, or **t** to complete the word that names each thing.

1. _____ oin   3. _____ oy

2. _____ oys   4. _____ oint

To Do At Home Think of words that have the "oi" sound. Write your words and show them to someone at home.

Decoding Skills: Vowel Sounds /oi/oi, oy   Copyright © by McGraw-Hill, Inc.   **27**

Name

"The Birds Take a Fall Trip," pages 66–73

Vowel Sounds

The letters **ow** or **ou** can stand for the **ow** sound in **now** or **loud**.

Write **ou** or **ow** to complete the word that names each picture.

1. t _____ n   4. s _____ th

2. cl _____ ds   5. h _____ se

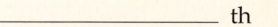

3. d _____ n   6. m _____ se

To Do At Home Clouds and rain stop birds from flying south. Make a drawing that shows what clouds and rain stop you from doing. Show it to someone at home.

28 Copyright © by McGraw-Hill, Inc.   **Decoding Skills: Vowel Sounds /ow/ow, ou**

Name

"The Birds Take a Fall Trip," pages 66–73

Consonant Sounds

The letter **s** can stand for the **z** sound, as in *is* or *has*.

Write the word that has the **z** sound to complete each sentence.

1. A bird _____ south when it gets cold.
         walks   flies

2. Birds _____ the sun to find their way.
     use   see

3. If a bird flies when there are clouds, it can _____ its way.
     show   lose

4. The trip can take many, many _____ .
         days   nights

To Do At Home Think of words in which **s** has the **z** sound. Write your words and show them to someone at home.

Decoding Skills: Consonant Sounds /z/s Copyright © by McGraw-Hill, Inc.

Name

"The Birds Take a Fall Trip," pages 66–73

Inflectional Endings

The **-er** ending compares two people or things.
The **-est** ending compares more than two people or things.

My dog runs *fast*.
Your dog runs *faster* than my dog.
Pablo's dog runs *fastest* of all.

Add **-er** or **-est** to complete the word in each sentence.

1. The eagle is fast _____ than the chicken.

2. But the goose can fly a long _____ way than the eagle.

3. Of all the birds, the eagle is the strong _____ .

4. A swallow can move quick _____ than a goose.

To Do At Home To how many words can you add the **-er** and **-est** endings? Make a list of these words. Show your list to someone at home.

30 Copyright © by McGraw-Hill, Inc.

Decoding Skills: Inflectional Endings -er, -est

Name

"The Birds Take a Fall Trip," pages 66–73

Apostrophe

The **s** at the end of **birds** makes the word mean "more than one."

To show that the birds own something, put an **apostrophe** (') after the **s**.

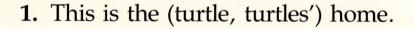

This is the bird**s'** home.

Put a line under the word that means "more than one owns it."

1. This is the (turtle, turtles') home.

2. This is the (bears', bear's) home.

3. This is the (owl's, owls') home.

4. This is the (frogs', frog's) home.

To Do At Home Draw a picture of some ducks in the water. Write this sentence under your picture: **This is the ducks' home.** Show your picture to someone at home. Tell why you used an apostrophe.

Study Skills: Apostrophe

Name

"The Birds Take a Fall Trip," pages 66–73

Words from the Story

Read the words in the box. Then write the word that goes with each picture.

clouds	rain	goose	point	stars
over	swallows	been	lose	south

1. _____

3. _____

2. _____

4. _____

To Do At Home Draw a picture of where the birds go in winter. Show your picture to someone at home.

32 Copyright © by McGraw-Hill, Inc.

Words from the Story

Name

"The Birds Take a Fall Trip," pages 66–73

Understanding the Story

Write the correct word to complete each sentence about "The Birds Take a Fall Trip."

1. Birds know that it is time to go when _____

   _____

   it is not as _____ as it has been.

   warm   cold

   _____

   _____

2. Birds may look at the _____
   to find the way.   sun   rain

   _____

   _____

3. Swallows do not fly at _____ .

   day   night

4. Some people put out _____

   _____

   _____ for birds that do not go south.

   books   seed

To Do At Home Birds fly south to stay warm.
Draw a picture that shows how you stay warm in
winter. Show your picture to someone at home.

Understanding the Story

Copyright © by McGraw-Hill, Inc. **33**

Name

"The Birds Take a Fall Trip," pages 66–73

Vowel Sounds

The letters **oi** and **oy** can stand for the **oi** sound in **point** and **boy**.

Write the word that has the **oi** sound to complete each sentence.

_____

– – – – – – – – – – –

1. Two _____ hear a call from the sky.

    dogs   boys

_____

– – – – – – – – – – – – – –

2. They _____ at the dark V in the clouds.

    point   look

_____

– – – – – – – – – – – –

3. What _____ it would be to fly!

    fun   joy

To Do At Home Make a list of five things that you think would be a joy to do. Show your list to someone at home.

34 Copyright © by McGraw-Hill, Inc.

Decoding Skills: Vowel Sounds /oi/oi, oy

Name

"The Birds Take a Fall Trip," pages 66–73

Vowel Sounds

The letters **ow** and **ou** can stand for the **ow** sound in **now** and **loud**.

Think of the best word to complete each line. Write **ou** or **ow** to complete the word.

1. If every animal in the _____

   t _____ n could fly,

2. You might see a horse or a _____

   m _____ se in the sky,

3. Or a bear in the _____

   cl _____ ds!

4. Those animals might never want _____

   to come d _____ n!

To Do At Home Draw a picture of what you might see if every animal could fly. Show your picture to someone at home.

Decoding Skills: Vowel Sounds /ow/ow, ou   Copyright © by McGraw-Hill, Inc.   **35**

Name

"The Birds Take a Fall Trip," pages 66–73

Inflectional Endings

The **-er** ending compares two people or things.

The **-est** ending compares more than two people or things.

       Winter is *cold*.

       Winter is *colder* than fall.

       Winter is the *coldest* time of all.

Write **-er** or **-est** to complete the word in each sentence.

1. The days are warm _____ now than in winter.

2. Each day is long _____ than the last.

3. Now the birds in the south need a cold _____ place to be.

4. The fast _____ bird will get there first.

To Do At Home Use the words **faster**, **older**, and **strongest** to tell about your friends. Tell someone at home about these friends of yours.

36 Copyright © by McGraw-Hill, Inc.

Decoding Skills: Inflectional Endings

Name

"Sea Frog, City Frog," pages 74–83

Words from the Story

Write the right word from the box to finish each sentence.

frowned	legs	nose	tall	side
hold	heads	lived	their	other

1. One little pig _____ in the woods.

2. The _____ little pig was from the city.

3. Two pigs sat by the _____ _____ of a rock and talked.

4. Then they went back to _____ own homes.

To Do At Home Which do you like better, the woods or the city? Draw a picture that shows the place you like. Show your picture to someone at home.

Words from the Story

Copyright © by McGraw-Hill, Inc. 37

Name

"Sea Frog, City Frog," pages 74–83

Understanding the Story

Read each question about "Sea Frog, City Frog."
Then write the answer on the lines.

1. What did Sea Frog want to see?

2. What did City Frog want to see?

3. Where do the frogs meet?

4. Where do the frogs go
when they leave the hill?

To Do At Home Find a picture of a place that
you would like to see. Show the picture to
someone at home. Tell why you want to go there.

38 Copyright © by McGraw-Hill, Inc.

Understanding the Story

Name

"Sea Frog, City Frog," pages 74–83

Making Comparisons

To *compare* means to tell how things are different. To compare two things, add **-er**. To compare more than two things, add **-est**. Read what the children are saying.

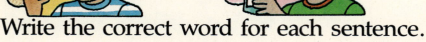

This is cold. This is colder. This is coldest of all!

Write the correct word for each sentence.

1. My bike is _____ than yours.
   newest   newer

2. Mr. Long is the _____ man in town.
   older   oldest

3. I will get there _____ than you.
   soonest   sooner

To Do At Home Use each of these words in a sentence: **quick, quicker, quickest**. Show your sentences to someone at home.

Comprehension Skills: Making Comparisons

Name

"Sea Frog City Frog," pages 74–83

Consonant Sounds

The letter **s** can stand for the **z** sound, as in **has** or **bears**.

Circle the word in each pair in which **s** has the **z** sound.

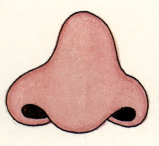

1. nose

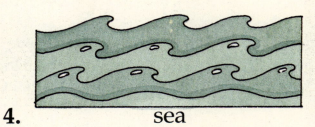

4. sea

2. star

5. leaves

3. grass

6. clothes

To Do At Home The birds take a trip south every fall. Where would you like to go on a trip? Draw a picture of where you would like to go. Show your picture to someone at home.

Decoding Skills: Consonant Sounds /z/s

Name

"Sea Frog, City Frog," pages 74–83

Apostrophe

sisters

the sisters' game

The **s** makes the word mean "more than one." The **apostrophe (')** after the **s** means "more than one owns it."

Write the word that means "more than one owns it."

_____

1. the _____ hats

boy's   boys'

_____

2. the _____ rings

kings'   king's

_____

3. the _____ home

horse's   horses'

To Do At Home Write this word in a sentence: **elephants'**. Tell about something the elephants own. Show your sentence to someone at home.

Study Skills: Apostrophe s'

Name

"Not THIS Bear," pages 86–97

Summarizing

A **summary** is a sentence that tells what the whole story is about. Read this story.

We like our bus ride to school. We sing songs. We talk to our friends. We wave to people.

Here is a **summary** of the story:

We have fun on the bus.

Read each story. Then put a line under the best summary.

1. Winter is over. You can tell! Birds sing again. Frogs jump. Seeds grow. Trees look green.
   a. You can tell that winter is over.
   b. Birds eat seeds.
   c. Frogs like warm days.

2. Mom and Dad have bikes. My bike is not so big. Sam's bike is very, very little.
   a. I like to ride my bike.
   b. Sam is a baby.
   c. We all have bikes.

To Do At Home Draw a picture. Write one sentence to tell what your picture is about. Show your picture to someone at home.

42 Copyright © by McGraw-Hill, Inc.

Comprehension Skills: Summarizing

Name

"Not This Bear," pages 86–97

Digraphs

The letters **th** stand for the beginning sound in *that* and the ending sound in *with*.

The letters **wh** stand for the beginning sound in *when*.

Write **th** or **wh** to complete the word that names each picture.

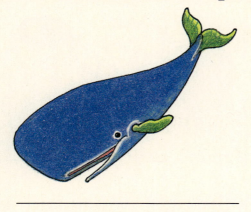 

1. _____ ale   3. _____ ree

 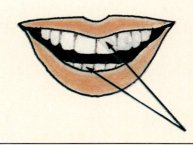

2. _____ eels   4. tee _____

To Do At Home Make a list of other words that have the **th** or **wh** sound. Show your list to someone at home.

Decoding Skills: Consonant Digraphs *th, wh*

Name

"Not THIS Bear" pages 86–97

Spelling Changes

Some words end in a **consonant** and **y**: ba**b**y.

Before you add **-es**, change the **y** to **i**: bab**ies**.

Put a line under the word that shows the right way to add **-es**.

1. berry

   a. berrys   b. berries

2. puppy

   a. puppies   b. puppys

3. library

   a. librarys   b. libraries

4. city

   a. citys   b. cities

To Do At Home Write a sentence using the word **babies**. Show your sentence to someone at home.

44   Copyright © by McGraw-Hill, Inc.   **Decoding Skills: Spelling Changes** *y* to *i*

Name
"Not THIS Bear," pages 86–97

Strategy Builder: Fantasy

Read the story. Use the notes in blue to learn more about make-believe stories. Then answer the questions.

    Some people have dogs for pets. Some people have cats for pets. Not many people have pet bears. But we do.

    Bob is our big pet bear. Most pets are a lot of work. But Bob is a big help. Bob likes to do the dishes at our house. He also keeps his room clean.

    Bob went to school. He can read and write. He likes to read stories to us at night. "When you are all in bed, I will start to read," Bob will say. "But your hands and faces have to be clean first!"

Look at what the bear can do.

Think about if a real bear can be like this.

1. Does this story seem real at first?

_____

_____

(Continued)

Strategy Builder: Fantasy

Copyright © by McGraw-Hill, Inc.   45

Name

"Not THIS Bear," pages 86–97

Strategy Builder: Fantasy *(Continued)*

2. What first tells you that the story is a fantasy?

3. Name one other thing that tells you that the story is a fantasy.

To Do At Home If you could have any animal for a pet, what would it be? Draw a picture that shows what it might be like to have this pet around your house.

Name

"Not THIS Bear," pages 86–97

Words from the Story

Write the word from the box that tells what the words on the left say.

| snow | spoon | trick | lapped | which |
| furry | clever | cousin | done | soup |

1. how the puppy ate his water

_____

2. you use it to eat with

_____

3. like an animal's warm coat

_____

4. hot food you eat with a spoon

_____

To Do At Home Draw a picture of a furry animal. Show your picture to someone at home.

Words from the Story

Name

"Not THIS Bear" pages 86–97

Understanding the Story

Read the sentences about "Not THIS Bear." Write **1** by what happens first. Write **2** by what happens next. Write **3** by what happens after that. Write **4** by what happens last. Then answer the question.

_____

_____ Herman reaches Aunt Gert's porch.

_____ A bear takes Herman's furry hat and coat.

_____ Herman takes the bus to see Aunt Gert.

_____ Herman stands on his head.

◇ **STRATEGY BUILDER**

Could this story happen in real life?

_____

_____

To Do At Home Draw a picture that shows the bears getting up after their winter sleep. Show your picture to someone at home.

48   Copyright © by McGraw-Hill, Inc.

Understanding the Story

Name

"Not THIS Bear" pages 86–97

Spelling Changes

Some words end in a consonant and y. Before you add **-es, -ed, -er,** or **-est,** change the **y** to **i.**

cry   **cr**i**es**   **cr**i**ed**   happy   happ**i**er   happ**i**est

Change **y** to **i.** Add the ending. Write the new word.

1. sky
(add **-es**)

2. carry
(add **-ed**)

3. furry
(add **-er**)

4. funny
(add **-est**)

To Do At Home Write a sentence for each word: **hungrier, hungriest.** Show your sentences to someone at home.

Decoding Skills: Spelling Changes y to i

Copyright © by McGraw-Hill, Inc.   49

Name

"Fish Story," pages 98–108

Words from the Story

Write the right word from the box to finish each sentence.

| story | loud | please | swam | thank |
| tie | ketchup | pretty | world | hungry |

1. I will tell you a _____ about a pig.

2. He wanted to see the _____ .

3. He swam in a _____ lake.

4. But he came home when he got _____ !

To Do At Home Pick two words you learned from this story. Write a sentence using each word. Show your sentences to someone at home.

50   Copyright © by McGraw-Hill, Inc.

Words from the Story

Name

"Fish Story," pages 98–108

Understanding the Story

Which sentence tells about "Fish Story"? Underline the answer. Then answer the question.

1. Little Fish wants to see the world.
   Big Cat wants to see the world.

2. Big Cat takes Little Fish to his house.
   Big Cat takes Little Fish to the sea.

3. Big Cat wants to help Little Fish.
   Big Cat wants to cook Little Fish.

4. Little Fish tells Big Cat about an old bike.
   Little Fish tells Big Cat about a bigger fish.

5. Big Cat puts Little Fish back in the pond.
   Big Cat puts Little Fish back in the pot.

◆ **STRATEGY BUILDER**

How do you know Little Fish is not a real fish?

_____

_____

_____

_____

To Do At Home Make up a story that tells how Big Cat might try to trick Little Fish. Tell your story to someone at home.

Understanding the Story

Name

"Fish Story" pages 98–108

Summarizing

A **summary** is a sentence that tells what the whole story is about. Read each story. Then underline the sentence that tells what the story is about.

1. Ben has a bird. Len has a cat. Sue and Pam have dogs. Dan has three little fish.
   a. Fish make good pets.
   b. All the children have pets.
   c. The children take pets to school.

2. We took some food. We took a blanket. We got in the car. Away we went to the sea! We had a good day.
   a. We like to eat good food.
   b. We had a day at the sea.
   c. We have a big car.

To Do At Home Play Story-Quiz. Tell in one sentence what a story is about. Have someone at home guess the name of the story. Then ask that person to summarize another story for you to guess.

52 Copyright © by McGraw-Hill, Inc.

COMPREHENSION SKILLS: Summarizing

Name

"Fish Story," pages 98–108

Digraphs

The letters **th** stand for the beginning sound in **that** and the ending sound in **with**.

The letters **wh** stand for the beginning sound in **when**.

Write **th** or **wh** to complete the words in the sentences.

1. Big Cat _____ inks he has a big fish.

2. But that is no fish down _____ ere!

3. _____ at is it then?

4. It feels like a _____ale!

To Do At Home Draw pictures of things that begin with **th** or **wh**. Have someone at home guess what the things are.

Decoding Skills: Consonant Digraphs **th, wh**

Copyright © by McGraw-Hill, Inc.   53

Name

Part Two: Far Away

Think about the stories you read. Use what you know about the stories to write sentences about the ideas on the page.

1. How nice it would be to go on a trip far away. Sometimes I think I would like to go to

2. No place is too far for me to go when I pretend I am

To Do At Home Think of a title for each story.
Read your title and story to someone at home.

54 Copyright © by McGraw-Hill, Inc.

Creative Writing

Name

"What Will the Weather Be?" pages 120–127

Main Idea and Supporting Details

Some stories have a main idea sentence. The sentence tells the most important idea in the story. The other sentences tell things that back up the main idea.

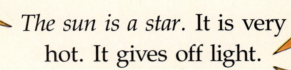

The sun is a star. It is very hot. It gives off light.

Read the stories. Put a line under the main idea sentence in each one.

1. A train has many cars on it. Some cars carry things. Some cars carry people. The first car pulls the train.

2. Many animals live by the water. Birds live there. So do frogs and turtles. Fish swim in the waves.

To Do At Home Write a story about an animal. Use a main idea sentence. Show your story to someone at home. Point to the main idea sentence.

Comprehension Skills: Main Idea and Supporting Details

Name

"What Will the Weather Be?" pages 120–127

Vowel Sounds

The letter **o** can have the **o** sound in **off**.

Write the word that has the **o** sound in **off** to complete each sentence.

1. The _____ runs to the house.

           mouse   dog

2. There is a _____ wind.

           loud   strong

3. Soon it will rain _____ and hard.

           good   long

To Do At Home Draw a picture that shows the weather that you like the best. Show your picture to someone at home.

Copyright © by McGraw-Hill, Inc.

Decoding Skills: Vowel Sounds /ô/o

Name

"What Will the Weather Be?" pages 120–127

Vowel Sounds

The letters **ew** can have the **you** sound in **few**.
The letters **ue** can have the **ooh** sound in true.

Write the word that has the **you** or **ooh** sound to complete each sentence.

1. It is the start of a _____ day.
   new   next

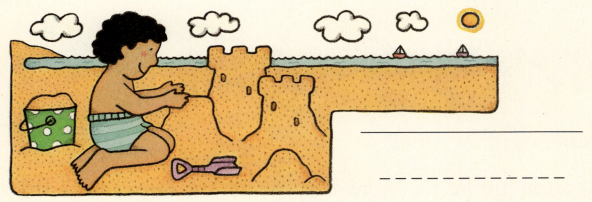

2. The sun is hot and the sky is _____ .
   blue   buy

3. Is it _____ _____ that people like this weather best?
   so   true

To Do At Home Some people look at plants and animals to find out what the weather will be. Draw a picture that shows how you find out the weather. Show your picture to someone at home.

Decoding Skills: Vowel Sounds /yu/ü/ew, /ü/ue

Name

"What Will the Weather Be?" pages 120–127

Antonyms and Synonyms

Some words have opposite meanings. These words are called **antonyms**.

little   big   sad   happy

Some words have almost the same meaning. These words are called **synonyms**.

little   small   hop   jump

1. Put a line under the word that means the **opposite** of the word in dark print.

   a. **out**   in   over   c. **up**   down   on

   b. **stay**   rest   go   d. **first**   three   last

2. Put a line under the word that means almost the **same** as the word in dark print.

   a. **every**   all   no   c. **fast**   quick   slow

   b. **tell**   sleep   say   d. **go**   stop   leave

To Do At Home Draw a picture of a place where everything is the opposite of the way things really are. Maybe you would walk on your hands! Show your picture to someone at home. Tell about it.

58 Copyright © by McGraw-Hill, Inc.   **Vocabulary Skills: Antonyms and Synonyms**

Name

"What Will the Weather Be?" pages 120–127

Words from the Story

Write the word from the box that means the *opposite* of each word on the left.

| country | different | few | these | off |

1. same _____

2. city _____

3. on _____

4. many _____

To Do At Home Think of some opposite words that you can act out. Act them out for someone at home. Can that person guess your opposite words?

Words from the Story

Copyright © by McGraw-Hill, Inc.   59

Name _____

What Will the Weather Be?" pages 120–127

Understanding the Story

Write the correct word to complete each sentence about "What Will the Weather Be?"

1. You can tell it will be cold when _____

   _____ stand close together.

       sheep   ducks

2. In cold weather some wild animals come down _____

   from the _____ .

       hills   trees

3. If the leaves of some plants turn in, you know the _____

   weather will be very _____ .

       warm   cold

To Do At Home Keep a weather chart for a week. Draw pictures to show if the weather is sunny, rainy, snowy, cloudy, or windy. Show your chart to someone at home.

Name

"What Will the Weather Be?" pages 120–127

Vowel Sounds

The letter **o** can have the **o** sound in **off**.

Write the word from the sentence that has the **o** sound in **off**.

1. We hear the song of the birds.

   ----

2. The dog wants to run up the hill.

   ----

3. The sun is too strong for the ice.

   ----

4. The long winter is over at last.

To Do At Home What time of year do you like the best? Draw a picture that shows what you like best about this time. Show it to someone at home.

Name

"What Will the Weather Be?" pages 120–127

Vowel Sounds

The letters **ew** can have the **you** sound in **few**. The letters **ue** can have the **ooh** sound in **true**.

Write the word with the **ew** or **ue** sound that names each picture.

1. _____

read   news

3. _____

stew   dish

2. _____

glue   paint

4. _____

blue   green

To Do At Home What words can you think of with the **ew** or **ue** sounds? Make a list of these words. Show your list to someone at home.

62 Copyright © by McGraw-Hill, Inc.   **Decoding Skills: Vowel Sounds /yü, ü/ew, ue**

Name

"Down the Hill," pages 128–137

Words from the Story

Write the right word from the box to finish each sentence.

| sled | upon | true | quit | pants |
| myself | behind | ready | laughed | great |

1. Pat and Sam went for a ride on a _____ .

2. Sam sat _____ his friend Pat.

3. They thought the ride was _____ .

To Do At Home Pick two words you learned from this story. Draw a picture to show what they are. Show your picture to someone at home.

Words from the Story

Copyright © by McGraw-Hill, Inc.   63

Name

"Down the Hill," pages 128–137

Understanding the Story

Read each question about "Down the Hill." Then write the answer on the lines.

1. Where is Toad when Frog comes to his house?

2. What do Frog and Toad ride on down the hill?

3. Who falls off first?

4. Who tells Toad that his friend is not behind him?

5. How does Toad feel when Frog is not there?

To Do At Home Make a list of things that you like to do in winter. Show your list to someone at home.

64 Copyright © by McGraw-Hill, Inc.

Understanding the Story

Name

"Down the Hill" pages 128–137

Main Ideas and Supporting Details

Some stories have a main idea sentence. The sentence tells the most important idea in the story. The other sentences back up the main idea. Read the story below.

The boys are playing. One boy kicks the ball. One boy runs after it. One boy kicks the ball back.

1. Which sentence tells the main idea? Copy it.

2. Copy a sentence that backs up the main idea.

To Do At Home Use this main idea sentence to begin a story: I like to play. Add two more sentences to back up your main idea. Show your story to someone at home.

Comprehension Skills: Main Idea and Supporting Details

Name

"Down the Hill" pages 128–137

Antonyms and Synonyms

Antonyms are words with almost the opposite meanings.

slow   fast

Synonyms are words with almost the same meanings.

fast   quick

1. Circle the antonym for the first word in dark print. Then copy the antonym for the next word in dark print.
   a. **yes**   no   well   b. **day**   sun   night

   _____

   _____

2. Circle the synonym for the first word in dark print. Then copy the synonym for the next word in dark print.
   a. **boat**   sea   ship   b. **little**   small   big

   _____

   _____

To Do At Home Ask someone at home to help you find synonyms for these words: **near, stop, every**.

66   Copyright © by McGraw-Hill, Inc.   **Vocabulary Skills: Antonyms and Synonyms**

Name

"The Ant and the Dove," pages 140–147

Consonant Sounds

The letter **g** can have the **j** sound, as in **cage**.

Circle each word in which **g** has the **j** sound.

1. bridge
2. giant
3. eagle
4. frog
5. dog
6. giraffe
7. game
8. engine
9. goat

To Do At Home How many other words can you list that have a **g** with the **j** sound? Show your list to someone at your home.

Decoding Skills: Consonant Sounds /j/g

Name

"The Ant and the Dove" pages 140–147

Context Clues

To find the meaning of a word, study the words around it. Read this sentence:

   Dad and I fixed the engine of the car.

You can tell from the sentence that engine means

 not

Circle the picture that shows the meaning of the word in dark print.

1. My friend **waves** to me.

a.

b.

2. Mother **rocks** the baby.

a.

b.

3. We made a **bed** for the plants.

a.

b.

To Do At Home Copy these sentences. Draw a picture to go with each one: 1. It is fall. 2. Don't fall down. Show your sentences and pictures to someone at home. Tell about the two meanings of fall.

68 Copyright © by McGraw-Hill, Inc.

Vocabulary Skills: Context Clues

Name

"The Ant and the Dove" pages 140–147

Skill: Referents

Look at the underlined words. They tell about the same word as the word in dark print.

I like <u>Jane</u>. **She** is my friend.

<u>Jane</u> gave **her** dog some food.

Put a line under the word that tells about the same thing as the word in dark print.

1. Sam has a bird. **He** feeds the bird.

2. Mary gave **her** cats some fish.

3. Mary said **she** likes the cats.

4. The man gave **his** elephant some berries.

5. The man pets the elephant and talks to **him**.

To Do At Home Write one sentence using both these words: **he**, **his**. Show your sentence to someone at home.

Vocabulary Skills: Referents

Name

"The Ant and the Dove" pages 140–147

Alphabetizing

You can put words in ABC order. Look at the first letter of each word. Think about the order of the letters in the alphabet. Then list the words that way. These words are in alphabetical order:

ant
elephant
giraffe

Put a line under the word on the right that makes each list have alphabetical order.

1. ask
   _____ can   please   find
   did

2. cubs
   _____ elves   here   all
   feet

3. six
   _____ kittens box   then
   wet

To Do At Home Think of three friends whose names begin with a different letter. List the names in alphabetical order. Show your list to someone at home.

70 Copyright © by McGraw-Hill, Inc.   Study Skills: Alphabetizing

Name

"The Ant and the Dove," pages 140–147

Comprehension Builder: Predicting Outcomes

Read the story. Use the notes in blue to help you predict the outcome of the story. Then answer the questions.

A giant tree stood next to a lake. The tall tree looked down on the little animals and plants around it. "I am not like you," said the tree. "I am big and strong."

In bad weather, the animals always ran away. The grass always fell down to get out of the wind. The tree laughed at this. "I am so big and strong," it said to the grass. "I would never fall down the way you do."

Look at how sure the tree is of itself.

The grass looked up at the tree. "Time will tell," said the grass. "Time will tell."

Think about what you know about storms.

One day a storm came. It was a storm like no other storm before.

The animals ran to hide. The grass got down out of the way. The tree did not like this storm at all. It began to move.

Think about why the tree does not like this storm.

(Continued)

Comprehension Builder: Predicting Outcomes

Copyright © by McGraw-Hill, Inc.   71

Name

"The Ant and the Dove," pages 140–147

Comprehension Builder: Predicting Outcomes

1. What do you think will happen next in the story?

2. What does the grass say that helps you guess what will happen next?

To Do At Home Draw a picture that shows how you think the story will end. Show it to someone at home.

72   Copyright © by McGraw-Hill, Inc.

Comprehension Builder: Predicting Outcomes

Name

"The Ant and the Dove," pages 140–147

Words from the Story

Write the word from the box that is the most like the words on the left.

| cage | bite | drop | beat | joy |
| dove | open | break | river | catch |

1. let fall _____

2. hit hard _____

3. kind of bird _____

4. grab something to keep it _____

To Do At Home Draw a picture of something that gives you joy. Write what the picture is, then show it to someone at home.

Name
"The Ant and the Dove," pages 140–147

Understanding the Story

Put a line under the sentence in each pair that tells about "The Ant and the Dove". Then answer the question.

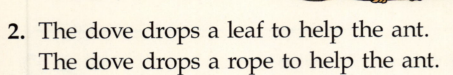

1. The ant can't fall.
   The ant can't swim.

2. The dove drops a leaf to help the ant.
   The dove drops a rope to help the ant.

3. A man catches the dove and puts her in a can.
   A man catches the dove and puts her in a cage.

4. The ant bites the man to help the dove.
   The ant grabs the man to help the dove.

5. This story is about helping those who help you.
   This story is about learning how to swim.

◆ **COMPREHENSION BUILDER**

Did you think the ant would help the dove? Why?
_____
_____
_____
_____

To Do At Home Make up a new story about the ant. Who helps her? What does the ant do for that person? Tell your story to someone at home.

Name

"The Ant and the Dove," pages 140–147

Consonant Sounds

The letter **g** can have the **j** sound, as in *cage*.

Write the word in which **g** has the **j** sound to complete each sentence.

1. It was a _____ day at the zoo.
          strange   great

2. The _____ sang some songs.
          eagle   giraffes

3. In their _____ the lions played the flute and drums.
          garden   cage

To Do At Home What would you like to see at the zoo? Draw a picture that shows it. Show your picture to someone at home.

Decoding Skills: Consonant Skills /j/g

Name _____

"The Ant and the Dove," pages 140–147

Context Clues

A word can have different meanings. To find the meaning of a word, study the words around it.

Read this sentence: She is a **star**.

In this sentence, you can tell that star means someone on TV, not something in the sky. Copy the words that tell the meaning of the word in dark print.

1. Did he **park** the car?
   a. put in a place   b. a place to play

_____

_____

2. I see a **fly**.
   a. move in the air   b. kind of bug

_____

_____

To Do At Home Think of a word that has two meanings. Write down the word and tell the two meanings to someone at home.

Vocabulary Skills: Context Clues

Name

"Just the Thing for Geraldine," pages 148–161

Words from the Story

Write the correct word to complete each sentence.

| cents | hurt | feel | third | choose |
| juggle | dance | brother | father | tried |

1. Fran took her little _____ Tim to "Fun Day."

2. Tim wanted to _____ around when a woman played the flute.

3. Fran _____ to catch a fish in the fishing game.

To Do At Home Pick two words you learned from this story. Write a sentence using each word. Show your sentences to someone at home.

Words from the Story

Copyright © by McGraw-Hill, Inc. 77

Name

"Just the Thing for Geraldine," pages 148–161

Understanding the Story

Write 1 in front of what happens first in "Just the Thing for Geraldine." Write 2 in front of what happens next. Write 3 in front of what happens last. Then answer the question.

_____ Geraldine brings home clay.

_____ Geraldine thinks of giving a juggling class.

_____ Geraldine goes to dance class.

◇ COMPREHENSION BUILDER

What do you know that helps you guess how the story will end?

_____

_____

_____

To Do At Home Think of something that you can do well. Show someone at home how to do it.

78   Copyright © by McGraw-Hill, Inc.

Understanding the Story

Name _____

"Just the Thing for Geraldine," pages 148–161

Referents

Look at the underlined word. It tells about the same thing as the word in dark print.

Sue likes the horse. <u>She</u> talks to him.

Write the word that tells about the word in dark print.

1. A **horse** is outside.
   He is eating plants. _____

2. The **girl** calls the horse.
   She gives the horse something to eat. _____

3. The horse thinks the **girl** is kind.
   The horse takes her for a ride. _____

4. The **horse** brings the girl back.
   The girl will ride him again. _____

To Do At Home Write one sentence using both these words: **she**, **her**. Show your sentence to someone at home.

Vocabulary Skills: Referents

Name

"Just the Thing for Geraldine," pages 148–161

Alphabetizing

Put a line under the first letter of each word in the box.
Then write the words in alphabetical order.

park	because	toad	nose	chase

To Do At Home Make an alphabet game. Write one letter on each piece of paper. Mix the pieces all up. Ask someone at home to help you put the letters in alphabetical order.

80   Copyright © by McGraw-Hill, Inc.

Study Skills: Alphabetizing

Name

Part Three: Learning

Think about the stories you read. Use what you know about the stories to write sentences about the ideas on this page.

1. I can find out what the weather will be if I

2. When the weather people on TV say that the weather will be bad, my friend and I plan

To Do At Home Think of a title for each story.
Read your title and story to someone at home.

Creative Writing

Copyright © by McGraw-Hill, Inc. **81**

Name

"A Nest of Wood Ducks," pages 170–177

Drawing Conclusions

A **conclusion** is an idea you have after you read a story.

Read this story.

We went to the park. We played ball.
We played games. We ate good food.

The conclusion you can reach is:

We did many things.

Read the stories. Put a line under the sentence that tells the conclusion.

1. The bird made a nest. She put
eggs in the nest. Little birds came
out of the eggs. The mother bird
took care of them.
   a. Bird nests are fun to look at.
   b. Mother birds care for their babies.

2. Days are fun. You play with your
friends. You go to school. Nights
are fun, too. People read stories to
you. Then you sleep with your
best blanket.
   a. Day and night have fun in them.
   b. Blankets are warm.

To Do At Home Draw a picture of little birds leaving the nest. Show your picture to someone at home.

82 Copyright © by McGraw-Hill, Inc.

Comprehension Skills: Drawing Conclusions

Name

"A Nest of Wood Ducks," pages 170–177

Following Directions

Look at what the boy is doing. He is *following directions*. The *directions* go 1, 2, 3.

1. Make a circle.

2. Put a small circle in it.

3. Put a red dot in the middle.

Follow these directions:
1. Make a big circle.
2. Make a little circle inside the big one.
3. Put a dot inside the little circle.

To Do At Home Give someone at home a piece of paper and a pencil. Ask that person to draw three things in order. Check to see if the person has followed your directions.

Study Skills: Following Directions

Name

"A Nest of Wood Ducks," pages 170–177

Words from the Story

Write the right word from the box to finish each sentence.

bugs	dives	goes	pass	hole
them	does	climb	pair	forest

1. Look at that rabbit go down that _____ !

2. The rabbit's home is in a _____ .

3. The rabbit _____ not want us to see where he lives.

To Do At Home Pick two words from this story and draw a picture to show each word. Show your pictures to someone at home.

84 Copyright © by McGraw-Hill, Inc.

Words from the Story

Name

"A Nest of Wood Ducks," pages 170–177

Understanding the Story

Read each question about "A Nest of Wood Ducks." Then write the answer on the lines.

1. What is a mother wood duck called?

2. What does the mother sit on in the nest?

3. What do the baby ducks learn to do first?

4. What do the baby ducks chase for food?

5. The hen stops taking care of the baby ducks when

To Do At Home Draw a picture of a tree and show an animal that lives there. Share your picture with someone at home.

Understanding the Story

Copyright © by McGraw-Hill, Inc.   **85**

Name

"A Nest of Wood Ducks," pages 170–177

Following Directions

Directions tell you what to do. They tell the order in which to do things. The order goes 1, 2, 3.

Look at the picture.

Tell Donna what to do. Put the steps in 1, 2, 3 order.

Go out.	Get up.	Put on clothes.

1. _____

2. _____

3. _____

To Do At Home Draw three pictures that show how to make something good to eat. Put your pictures in 1, 2, 3, order. Show your picture-directions to someone at home.

86 Copyright © by McGraw-Hill, Inc.

Study Skills: Following Directions

Name

"City Magic," pages 178–185

Words from the Story

Read the words in the box. Write the word next to each picture that names the picture.

hang	dig	four	window
flower	full	three	kind	buy

1.

2.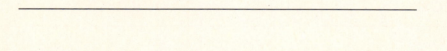

3.

To Do At Home Draw a picture of three different kinds of flowers. Show your picture to someone at home.

Name

"City Magic," pages 178–185

Understanding the Story

Put 1 by what happened first in "City Magic." Put 2 by what happened next. Put 3 by what happened after that. Put 4 by what happened last.

_____ Grandma shows the flowers in her window.

_____ Water the soil with care.

_____ Put the pot and dish near a window.

_____ Fill the pot with soil so that it is not quite full.

To Do At Home Draw a picture of something else that grows. Show your picture to someone at home.

88

Understanding the Story

Name

"City Magic," pages 178–185

Drawing Conclusions

After you read a story, you reach a **conclusion** about it. That is, the story leaves you with an idea. Read this story.

> Names! Names! Names! Ben wants to be called Benny. Cindy wants to be called Deedee. John Jones wants to be called J. J.

The conclusion you can reach is: Some people want new names.

Copy the sentence that tells the conclusion of the story.

> We went to the woods. We saw many birds. Some are here all the time. Some stay here just when it is warm. Some birds just fly by on their way to some other place.

1. Birds like warm days. 2. Birds stay and go.
3. Birds are pretty. 4. I like birds.

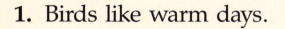

_____

_____

_____

To Do At Home Draw a picture of a bird you know. Write a sentence that tells something you know about this bird. Show your picture to someone at home.

Comprehension Skills: Drawing Conclusions

Name
"The Turnip," pages 188–197

Cause and Effect

Some stories let you know why someone does something.

Read this story.

   Tina put a plant in the garden. "It is too little," said Jane. "It will not grow."
   "It is too cold out," said Billy. "The plant will not grow."
   The plant got big. It got green. Tina was very happy. She jumped for joy.

Why did Tina jump for joy? The picture shows you why.

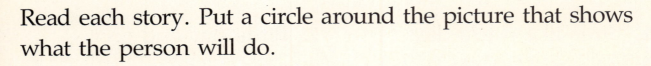

Read each story. Put a circle around the picture that shows what the person will do.

1. Bill fell down. He cut his hand.

2 My puppy ran away. Then I found it.

To Do At Home Write these sentences: **I was sad. Then someone gave me a big hug.** Draw a picture of how you would feel after the big hug. Show your sentences and your picture to someone at home.

Comprehension Skills: Cause and Effect

Name

"The Turnip," pages 188–197

Strategy Builder: Folk tales

Read the story. Use the side notes to help you learn more about folklore. Then answer the questions.

Fox always bothered the hens on the Brown farm. One night, Fox fell into a hole and could not get out.

The next day Farmer Brown found Fox. "Now I have you where I want you!" he said.

"No, this is where I want to be," said Fox. "This is a wishing hole."

"Wishing hole?" said the man. "What is that?"

Think about why Fox is being nice to Mr. Brown.

"Stand in this hole and make a wish," said Fox. "And it will come true."

Mr. Brown had one wish. So he jumped down into the hole. "What was your wish?" he asked Fox.

Look at how silly Farmer Brown is.

"I wished I could get out of this hole," said Fox. With that he jumped up on the head of the man. From there he jumped out of the hole. "Thanks, Farmer Brown," said Fox. "My wish just came true."

Think about how Fox tricks Farmer Brown.

Continued

Strategy Builder: Folk tales

Copyright © by McGraw-Hill, Inc. **91**

Name

"The Turnip," pages 188–197

Strategy Builder: Folk tales (Cont'd)

1. Who is silly in this folk tale?

2. What does Fox do in this folk tale that animals cannot do in real life?

3. What does Fox do to Mr. Brown that helps you know that this is a folk tale?

To Do At Home Make up a folk tale of your own. Use any kind of animals you want. Have one of the animals trick another. Tell your folk tale to someone at home.

92 Copyright © by McGraw-Hill, Inc.

Strategy Builder: Folk tales

Name

"The Turnip," pages 188–197

Words from the Story

Write the right word from the box to finish each sentence.

| prize | rich | girl | turnip | popped | our |

1. A _____ grows in the ground.

2. We have one in _____ _____ garden.

3. I showed it to a _____ _____ I know.

4. She says that it is so big, it could _____ win a _____ .

To Do At Home Draw a picture of something that grows in the ground. Show your picture to someone at home.

Words from the Story

Name

"The Turnip," pages 188–197

Understanding the Story

Write the correct word to complete each sentence about "The Turnip." Then answer the question.

1. The man thinks the turnip will make him

_____

_____

rich   fat

----

2. The man needs help to _____
the turnip.   take in   pull out

STRATEGY BUILDER

This folk tale is funny because many people must

_____

_____

_____

To Do At Home A turnip is a food that grows in the ground. Make a list of foods that grow on trees. Show your list to someone at home.

94   Copyright © by McGraw-Hill, Inc.

Understanding the Story

Name

"The Turnip," pages 188–197

Apostrophe

To show that one person or thing owns something, add an apostrophe (') and an **s**:

the boy's puppy

To show that more than one person or thing owns something, add an **s** and then an apostrophe (').

the boys' puppy

Look at each picture. Copy the word that tells about it.

1. the _____ treehouse

   a. girl's   b. girls'

2. the _____ bed
   a. cats'   b. cat's

3. the _____ nest

   a. birds'   b. bird's

To Do At Home Write this sentence: *This is the dogs' food.* Draw a picture to go with the sentence. Show your picture and sentence to someone at home.

Study Skills: Apostrophe's, s' Review   Copyright © by McGraw-Hill, Inc.   95

Name

"The Turnip," pages 188–197

Classifying

To **classify** means to put things together that are alike. Read the words in the box. Then write them in the group where they belong.

Mom	city	baby	Pete	farm	town

1. People

_____

_____

_____

2. Places

_____

_____

_____

To Do At Home Make a list of three things in your house. Draw a picture of each thing. Show your list to someone at home.

96   Copyright © by McGraw-Hill, Inc.

Comprehension Skill: Classifying (Review)

Name

"The Turnip," pages 188–197

Following Directions

Directions tell you what to do. They tell you in 1, 2, 3 order. Tim's car goes slowly. Read the directions in the box. Write them in order to show what Tim should do.

Call for help.	Stop the car.	Fix the car.

1. _____

2. _____

3. _____

To Do At Home Get a big piece of paper. Make a hat out of it. Then show someone at home how to make a paper hat.

Study Skills: Following Directions *Review*

Copyright © by McGraw-Hill, Inc. **97**

Name

"Farming," pages 198–207

Words from the Story

Write the right word from the box to finish each sentence.

ground	dug	mine	mess	tail
melons	potatoes	promise	whispered	roar

1. Dot said, "We will have to dig in the _____ to find the treasure."

2. She said, "You can dig, if you do _____ " not make a _____ .

3. So I _____ where she said to, but all we found was an old shoe!

To Do At Home Think of something you could find in the ground. Draw a picture. Show the picture to someone at home.

Name
"Farming," pages 198–207

Understanding the Story

Put a line under the sentence in each pair that tells about "Farming." Then answer the question.

1. Coyote never has melons.
   Coyote always has melons.

2. Badger works hard on his farm.
   Coyote works hard on his farm.

3. Badger does not keep his promise.
   Coyote does not keep his promise.

4. Badger gets the potatoes because they grow under the ground.
   Badger gets the melons because they grow under the ground.

5. Coyote has many melons that winter.
   Coyote has no melons that winter.

STRATEGY BUILDER

Which animal wants to trick the other in this folk tale?
_____
_____
_____

To Do At Home Tell someone at home the story of Coyote and Badger. Tell if you like the way it ends and why.

Understanding the Story

Name

"Farming," pages 198–207

Cause and Effect

Read each story. Copy the ending that tells why the person did something.

1. We moved to a new city. I was sad. Then I met Ben. We played in the park. We played games. I was happy because
   a. I had a new friend.   b. I like big cities.

2. The wind is strong. The snow falls. I put on my furry hat because
   a. I like to be funny.   b. I am cold.

To Do At Home Write this sentence: **I am happy.** Then draw a picture of what makes you happy. Show your sentence and picture to someone at home.

100 Copyright © by McGraw-Hill, Inc.

Comprehension Skills: Cause and Effect *Review*

Name

"Farming," pages 198–207

Contractions

In a **contraction,** two words are put together, but one letter is left out. An **apostrophe** (') takes the place of the missing letter.

Choose the **contraction** and write it in the blank.

_____

– –

1. I _____ go to the farm.
   a. did not   b. didn't

_____

– –

2. I _____ see the horse.
   a. couldn't   b. could not

_____

– – – – – – – – – – – – – – – –

3. _____ in a car.
   a. He is   b. He's

_____

– – – – – – – – – – – – – – – –

4. _____ time to go home.
   a. It's   b. It is

To Do At Home Write a sentence for each of these contractions: *hasn't, wouldn't*. Show your sentences to someone at home. Tell what two words each contraction stands for.

Study Skills: Contractions *Review*   Copyright © by McGraw-Hill, Inc.   **101**

Name

Part Four: Growing

Think about the stories you read. Use what you know about the stories to write sentences about the ideas on this page.

1. I like to see things grow. If I had a garden, I would

_____

2. I like to see animals grow. If I had my own zoo, I could see little

_____

To Do At Home Think of a title for each story.
Read your title and story to someone at home.

102 Copyright © by McGraw-Hill, Inc.

Creative Writing